A Pillar Box Red Publication

in association with

MATCH!
THE BEST FOOTBALL MAGAZINE!

BARCELONA ANNUAL 2019

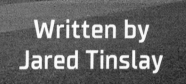

Written by
Jared Tinslay

Edited by
Stephen Fishlock

Designed by
Darryl Tooth

CONTENTS

SEASON REVIEW

We look back at Barça's 2017-18 campaign month by month, checking out their key moments, star players and more!

AUGUST

MEGA MOMENTS!

Rakitic battles with Marcelo

Barcelona's first competitive matches of the 2017-18 season didn't quite go as planned, with massive El Clasico rivals Real Madrid thrashing them out of sight 5-1 on aggregate in the Spanish Super Cup!

Sergi Roberto celebrates

Gaffer Ernesto Valverde's La Liga debut helped ease the Spanish Super Cup suffering! An own goal and a Sergi Roberto finish saw Barcelona easily beat a Real Betis side that didn't even manage a shot on target!

After striker Neymar joined PSG for a world-record £198 million on August 4, La Blaugrana bosses decided to splash some of that cash on Ousmane Dembele! The speedy France forward signed on August 28 for a fee that could rise to £135.5 million!

Dembele and Neymar join their new clubs

MAN OF THE MONTH!

LIONEL MESSI Leo's quality brace v Alaves took him past the 350 La Liga goals mark, but if it wasn't for a bit of bad luck, he would have got there even earlier. Messi hit the woodwork three times against Real Betis, and missed a penalty v Alaves as well!

DID YOU KNOW?

Paulinho made his Barcelona debut against Alaves, coming on in the 88th minute for Andres Iniesta.

BARCELONA'S RESULTS

Date	Comp	Home	Score	Away
13/08	SUC	Barcelona	1-3	Real Madrid
16/08	SUC	Real Madrid	2-0	Barcelona
20/08	LIGA	Barcelona	2-0	Real Betis
26/08	LIGA	Alaves	0-2	Barcelona

JANUARY

MEGA MOMENTS!

After drawing their first leg Copa del Rey last 16 clash 1-1 with Celta Vigo using a second-string side, Barça turned up the heat at the Nou Camp by bringing back the big guns! Two first-half Messi goals in two minutes set up a comfortable win.

Messi shows off his tekkers

BARCELONA'S RESULTS

04/01	CDR	Celta Vigo	1-1	Barcelona
07/01	LIGA	Barcelona	3-0	Levante
11/01	CDR	Barcelona	5-0	Celta Vigo
14/01	LIGA	Real Sociedad	2-4	Barcelona
17/01	CDR	Espanyol	1-0	Barcelona
21/01	LIGA	Real Betis	0-5	Barcelona
25/01	CDR	Barcelona	2-0	Espanyol
28/01	LIGA	Barcelona	2-1	Alaves

Barça hadn't won a league game in 11 years at Real Sociedad's ground, and things were looking bleak after the home side went 2-0 up after 34 minutes. But Los Cules battled back with Suarez curling a sublime lob to equalise!

Suarez gets two v Sociedad

Coutinho makes his bow

They met Espanyol in the Copa del Rey quarter-final and, after losing the first-leg 1-0, they needed another crazy Nou Camp comeback! Suarez and Messi saw them through, with Philippe Coutinho coming on for his debut.

MAN OF THE MONTH!

LIONEL MESSI 'The Flea' became the only La Liga player ever to score 25+ goals in each of the last ten seasons in all competitions, and assisted in five La Liga games in a row for the first time in his career!

DID YOU KNOW?

After signing Philippe Coutinho from Prem giants Liverpool in early January, Barça inserted a monster £355 million buy-out clause in his contract. Wow!

FEBRUARY

MEGA MOMENTS!

Coutinho celebrates

Barcelona took a one-goal lead into their Copa del Rey second-leg semi-final, and they sealed their place in the final with another victory at Valencia's Mestalla! Coutinho opened the scoring with his first goal for the club, before Rakitic made it two!

BARCELONA'S RESULTS

01/02	CDR	Barcelona	1-0	Valencia
04/02	LIGA	Espanyol	1-1	Barcelona
08/02	CDR	Valencia	0-2	Barcelona
11/02	LIGA	Barcelona	0-0	Getafe
17/02	LIGA	Eibar	0-2	Barcelona
20/02	CL	Chelsea	1-1	Barcelona
24/02	LIGA	Barcelona	6-1	Girona

Messi and Iniesta party

Chelsea were 15 minutes away from taking a 1-0 lead to the Nou Camp in the CL last 16, but Messi had other plans! It was actually Iniesta who made the goal, skipping past Azpilicueta before teeing up Leo to get an all-important away goal!

Suarez stole the show in Los Cules' thrashing of Girona, netting his first hat-trick of the season and heading home with the match ball! He took his tally up to 20 La Liga goals, just two behind Messi at that point!

Hat-trick hero Suarez

MAN OF THE MONTH!

PHILIPPE COUTINHO As well as helping to fire his side past Valencia to get to the Copa del Rey final, Coutinho also played a blinder against Girona, assisting one for Suarez and scoring a trademark screamer after cutting in from the left wing!

DID YOU KNOW?

Barcelona's 0-0 draw with Getafe was the first game in which they failed to score in La Liga in 2017-18!

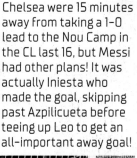

MARCH

MEGA MOMENTS!

600-up for lethal Leo

Footy wizard Messi curled a sublime first-half free-kick into the net against Atletico Madrid to bring up his 600th career goal for club and country! It also sent Los Cules eight points clear at the top of La Liga ahead of their opponents.

Barça got off to the best possible start in their CL second-leg clash with Chelsea, after Messi scored from a tight angle in the third minute. The Blues had some decent chances, but the result never really looked in doubt with Barcelona running out 3-0 winners.

Barça celebrate another big win

Barcelona were two goals down with three minutes to play against Sevilla! They pulled off a miraculous comeback, thanks to a Suarez half volley and a sweeping Messi strike to keep their unbeaten record alive!

Barça leave it late

MAN OF THE MONTH!

LIONEL MESSI Leo scored in every single game he played for Barcelona in March – he was rested for the Malaga match. He netted six goals in five games – and some of them were really crucial!

DID YOU KNOW?

Atletico only managed one shot on target in the whole match during their 1-0 loss at the Nou Camp!

BARCELONA'S RESULTS

Date	Comp	Home	Score	Away
01/03	LIGA	Las Palmas	1-1	Barcelona
04/03	LIGA	Barcelona	1-0	Atletico Madrid
10/03	LIGA	Malaga	0-2	Barcelona
14/03	CL	Barcelona	3-0	Chelsea
18/03	LIGA	Barcelona	2-0	Athletic Bilbao
31/03	LIGA	Sevilla	2-2	Barcelona

APRIL

MEGA MOMENTS!

Umtiti gets his first of the season

Barcelona broke the all-time La Liga unbeaten record against Valencia, thanks to another goal from Suarez and a header by France defender Samuel Umtiti! It marked their 39th league game without defeat, breaking a 38-year record. Wowzers!

Another trophy for Barça

Sevilla didn't stand a chance against Barcelona in the Copa del Rey final, with La Blaugrana's boys on top form! Iniesta put on a real show at the Wanda Metropolitano before announcing that he was leaving the club!

Messi scored his 46th career hat-trick against Deportivo, sealing the La Liga title with four games to spare at the Riazor! It was the perfect end to a special month for the club – bar the shock Champo League exit to Roma!

Unstoppable Messi

BARCELONA'S RESULTS

Date	Comp	Home	Score	Away
04/04	CL	Barcelona	4-1	Roma
07/04	LIGA	Barcelona	3-1	Leganes
10/04	CL	Roma	3-0	Barcelona
14/04	LIGA	Barcelona	2-1	Valencia
17/04	LIGA	Celta Vigo	2-2	Barcelona
21/04	CDR	Sevilla	0-5	Barcelona
29/04	LIGA	Deportivo	2-4	Barcelona

MAN OF THE MONTH!

LIONEL MESSI It has to be that man yet again! Two mind-blowing La Liga hat-tricks – one sealing the title – and a special display and goal in the Copa del Rey final against Sevilla, means Messi was once again the outstanding performer in April!

DID YOU KNOW?

It was against Leganes that Barcelona equalled Real Sociedad's 38-game unbeaten record – a feat they achieved across the 1978-79 and 1979-80 seasons!

Another El Clasico goal for Suarez

MAY

MEGA MOMENTS!

The final El Clasico of the season was an exciting encounter. Things got heated in the first half, and Sergi Roberto was sent off, but Barcelona still got a point with Suarez and Messi once again on target!

Just two games away from going the whole season unbeaten, Barça lost 5-4 in a crazy match against Levante! Even a sick Coutinho hat-trick couldn't rescue a point on a day that just wasn't to be for La Blaugrana!

Treble delight for Coutinho

The shock Levante loss couldn't take away from an incredible season for Barcelona, which was capped by a final day 1-0 victory over Real Sociedad where the hosts lifted the La Liga title at the Nou Camp!

Sergi Roberto gets his marching orders

Title number 25 for Barça

MAN OF THE MONTH!

ANDRES INIESTA He might not have played a full 90-minute match in his last month at the club, but Iniesta's farewell ceremony after the Real Sociedad match was a truly magic moment for the midfielder – and the club! Barcelona said goodbye to a legend.

DID YOU KNOW?

Sergi Roberto's red card against Real Madrid was his second sending-off of the season – he was the only Barcelona player to see red in La Liga in 2017-18!

BARCELONA'S RESULTS

06/05	LIGA	Barcelona	2-2	Real Madrid
09/05	LIGA	Barcelona	5-1	Villarreal
13/05	LIGA	Levante	5-4	Barcelona
20/05	LIGA	Barcelona	1-0	Real Sociedad

DOUBLE DELIGHT

Barcelona achieved a record-breaking double in 2017-18, including winning their 30th Copa del Rey trophy! Take a look at the numbers behind their awesome season...

400
There were 400 days between Barça's loss to Levante and their previous La Liga defeat in April 2017! They almost went the whole season unbeaten!

99
Barça scored 99 league goals –more than any La Liga side – and also hit the woodwork more than any team in Europe!

5-0
No Copa del Rey final has ever been won by more than a five-goal margin, and it had only ever happened twice before Barça's thrashing of Sevilla!

4
It was Los Cules' fourth consecutive Copa del Rey win, and their sixth in the last ten seasons! No team has ever won five trophies in a row!

40
Barcelona competed in their 40th Copa del Rey final – overtaking Real Madrid's record of 39!

34
After netting 34 La Liga goals, Lionel Messi pipped Mohamed Salah and Harry Kane to his fifth European Golden Shoe!

60%
No La Liga side kept the ball more than Los Cules – they averaged 60% possession in every match. Dominant!

WORDSEARCH

Can you find the names of these total Barcelona legends?

```
C W F T X X V C I V R K P P L H R Q L W B L U V U F U X L M
E F A O M K D L K C S V Y P E Q Q K Y J M W G G N I V K T M
F O N N S O X I C I I X E U I A W L M E P U Y O L Y N K Y G
E D K M D E F M V A D E Q C T Q Y Z Y B A Z X U D A B A Q X
A X L F E M S C J I Q I W D V A O T W Y W W X R R Y C V W G
U K G J P A V D B U R Z N Q M K K F O G U C T K I I K H W R
E E P S O N T V M N Q K W K U E F M Y E R K G S K K L R V O
Q B A A X B S L E A A Y D S U N S K W B D A A W Z K H O T N
V V U C H Z C Z M A L P R T J W J S F H V V F X Z X K M O A
Y J L A B D O U H G O I D O P C Z Z I I C X Q T N P U A R L
E N I S L A Z B Y I Z H P I B Q O V U S C H U S T E R R R D
J Q N T Q C Z I A E P B M C R A C O W Y W S Z S J U U I E I
T N O R C D H Z V Q W E N H I Y H W F Z A C F D O M T O S N
E C H O N Q G A F U I B L K G E K B K F Z C X D R A M W U H
M Z P O U F J R J F V R Z O T O O A P Z V Y L A A R G T S O
L R O E Y E Q R T G P O Q V J P D Q D K Z A Z K U A H R E L
Q R O M K G V E H A W V D N W Y X P I C V F B O J D N F L R
U C F A O B J T T M S H C S U L M D R I B P G C X O Z D N P
G C J N S T E A N P L X Y P G H N I R F A U M S O N I W K N
V Y N B N E E S K E N S V E U P M S A Z K B B I X A N H L N
O G E G Y K F Q R R R O U P R K N L N O E O E S L F I P U W
O O L N O Q I O A X C P N V R O O N O K R F V F A I E O I L
N A B K A D L W N S C E F O W I N Q I I O V B Z I Y S A V X
M H R J D U H A A D E W M T D I Z A J N M I P A W C T R E Z
C G X T S Z Q R U D A A E R Q A P H L I P S P B R M A L R H
P V E G R O R Z Q D A L A I Z L G Q X D T U K U D J J H T W
B Z Y U S A O N V J R U V D E N Y V A I O J C L N X U A H B
R E A N C Z X G R M G U W E R C E C V C R U Y F F Y Y A W F
L Y Q W S O R L L Z E G P V S W O Y I V Q N D C A X V A N I
D Y V K Q T P H X U P S R T V E Q G W N U M M W N F F T M F
```

Alves	Cruyff	Kocsis	Neeskens	Ronaldo
Amor	Enrique	Koeman	Paulino	Schuster
Bakero	Gamper	Krankl	Puyol	Stoichkov
Barjuan	Guardiola	Laudrup	Rivaldo	Torres
Carrasco	Iniesta	Maradona	Romario	Xavi
Castro	Kluivert	Messi	Ronaldinho	Zubizarreta

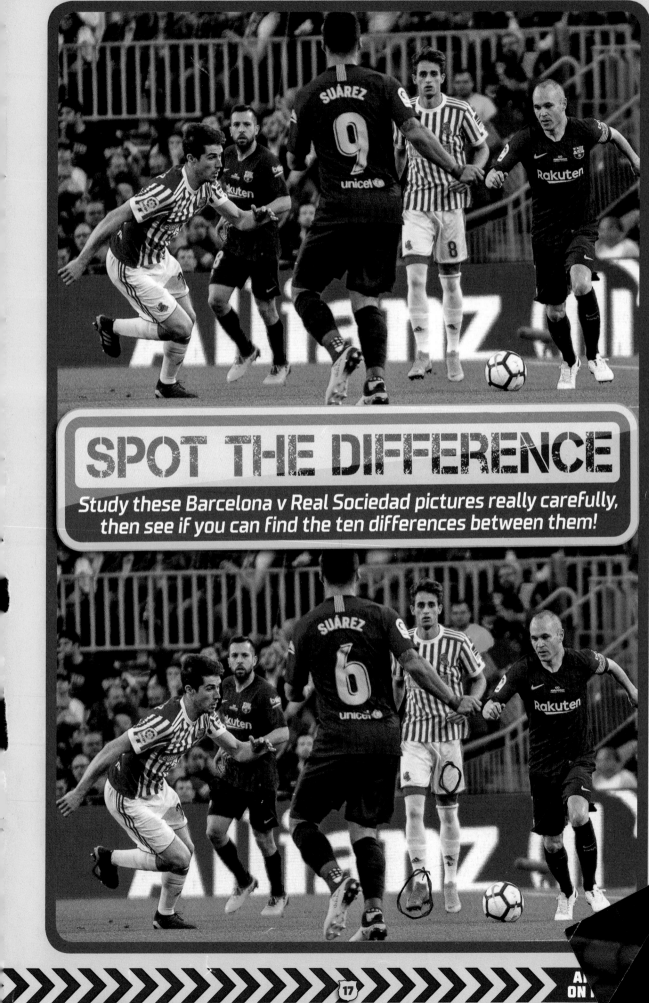

SPOT THE DIFFERENCE

Study these Barcelona v Real Sociedad pictures really carefully, then see if you can find the ten differences between them!

NOU CAMP IN NUMBERS

1957

The year the mega stadium was built!

1

It's the biggest stadium in Europe, and the second largest footy arena in the world!

£656

The price of an awesome VIP box season ticket in 2017-18!

99,354

The current capacity
of the Nou Camp!

105,000

The future capacity once it's
been redeveloped!

2021

The year the 'Nou
Camp Nou' will be
ready for action!

£500M

Roughly how much it'll
cost to expand the
current stadium!

2

Number of Champions
League finals it's
hosted – in 1989
and 1999!

120,000

The Nou Camp's record
attendance – in 1986
v Juventus!

COUTINHO
THE SAMBA STAR

The classy Brazilian is ready to take the creative reigns at Barça.

Philippe Coutinho's transfer to the Nou Camp in the 2018 winter window seemed a long time coming for Barcelona supporters. Liverpool already had rejected three big offers from the Catalan club the previous summer, and also the player's following transfer request. The Reds were absolutely desperate not to let their prized asset go – and who could blame them? In Coutinho, they had one of the best creative players in the Premier League – a footy superstar that could make magic happen with just a flick of his boot. That's why Barcelona were so keen to land him, and why they ended up paying such a large fee to convince Liverpool to part way with their top playmaker. If he hasn't already, surely it's only a matter of time before 'O Magico' wins the hearts of all La Blaugrana faithful...

BRITISH RECORD DEAL

The day before the 2018 January transfer window opened, an advert was revealed saying fans could get Coutinho's name printed on their Barça shirts – and on January 6, his record-breaking transfer was confirmed. The £105 million deal, rising to £142 million, made the Brazilian the third most expensive player in the world – and was the biggest fee a British club had ever received for a footballer!

THE FULL CIRCLE

Coutinho had actually stepped foot onto the Nou Camp pitch as a player before moving there – and not just for any club. It was for city rivals Espanyol, who he'd joined on loan in 2012 from Inter. The 19-year-old came off the bench just after the hour, and interestingly enough, made his Barcelona debut against Espanyol six years later – coming on as a sub again just after the hour!

REPLACING INIESTA

Barcelona lost Neymar to PSG in the summer of 2017, and also had an ageing Andres Iniesta unable to play as much football as he used to. For that reason, Coutinho was seen as the ideal signing. Not only does he have the quick feet, tricks and agility to dribble past a man like Neymar, he also has the vision, footy brain and passing ability to create goalscoring chances like Iniesta.

SAMBA FOOTSTEPS

There's something about Barça that seems to attract the best Brazilian ballers. In the past, football legends like Ronaldo, Ronaldinho, Rivaldo, Romario, Dani Alves and Neymar have all graced the Nou Camp pitch. Coutinho is the 33rd Samba star to represent the club, and history says he could go on to become an all-time club great. Los Cules will have their fingers crossed that he can!

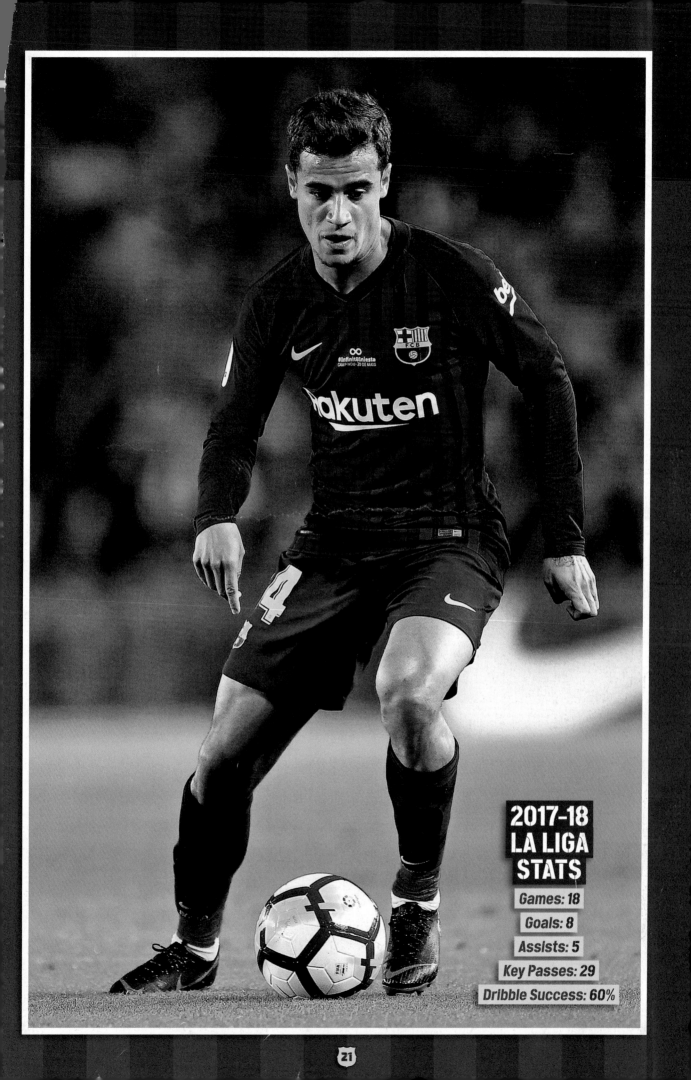

2017-18 LA LIGA STATS

Games: 18
Goals: 8
Assists: 5
Key Passes: 29
Dribble Success: 60%

LEO MESSI
100 GOALS

Last season, *LIONEL MESSI* became the fastest player to score 100 goals in the Champions League! This is how the BARÇA ledge did it...

GOAL 1

Barcelona 5 | 0 Panathinaikos

November, 2005 Messi's first ever CL goal was a bit special! The 18-year-old latched onto the ball in the area and then dinked it over the keeper's head, before tapping it into the net. It was a sign of the hot young talent's brilliance, and indeed, of things to come!

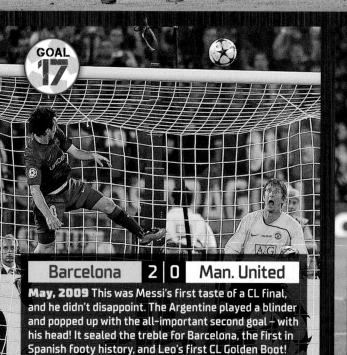

GOAL 14

Barcelona	5	2	Lyon

March, 2009 Having inherited the iconic No.10 shirt following Ronaldinho's departure, Messi established himself as the club's star player. He proved why with this incredible goal in the last 16, bamboozling three defenders, playing a lightning-quick one-two with Samuel Eto'o and stroking the ball into the net!

GOAL 17

Barcelona	2	0	Man. United

May, 2009 This was Messi's first taste of a CL final, and he didn't disappoint. The Argentine played a blinder and popped up with the all-important second goal – with his head! It sealed the treble for Barcelona, the first in Spanish footy history, and Leo's first CL Golden Boot!

GOAL 20

GOAL 21

Barcelona	4	0	Stuttgart

March, 2010 Off the back of a La Liga hat-trick, Leo went into this last 16 CL clash with huge confidence. He was the best player on the pitch by a mile, and scored two incredible long-range left-footed efforts – the first a piledriver, and the second an excellent low finish!

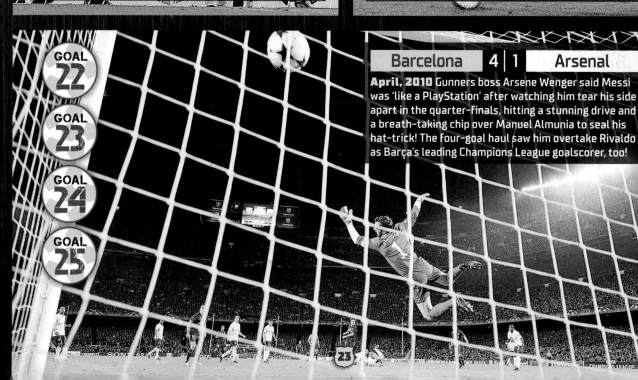

GOAL 22

GOAL 23

GOAL 24

GOAL 25

Barcelona	4	1	Arsenal

April, 2010 Gunners boss Arsene Wenger said Messi was 'like a PlayStation' after watching him tear his side apart in the quarter-finals, hitting a stunning drive and a breath-taking chip over Manuel Almunia to seal his hat-trick! The four-goal haul saw him overtake Rivaldo as Barça's leading Champions League goalscorer, too!

GOAL 26

GOAL 27

Barcelona	5	1	Panathinaikos

September, 2010 The Nou Camp fell silent in the 20th minute when the visitors took the lead, but it only took Leo 60 seconds to equalise. It was Messi's first goals since becoming Barça's all-time CL top scorer – and they came against the side his Euro journey started against!

GOAL 32

GOAL 33

Barcelona	3	1	Arsenal

March, 2011 Almunia was still having nightmares from their meeting the previous year, and things were only going to get worse! After being chipped in 2010, he was lobbed on the stroke of half-time in this match, before Leo netted a penalty to seal the win in the second half!

GOAL 35

GOAL 36

Real Madrid	0	2	Barcelona

April, 2011 This tense, bad-tempered El Clasico will always be remembered for one of the best goals the tournament's ever seen! After putting his side ahead, Messi then turned up the heat late on, skipping past four defenders and rolling it into the net. Pure class!

GOAL 37

Barcelona	3	1	Man. United

May, 2011 In a repeat of the 2009 CL final, Barça met United at Wembley. The game was all-square in the 54th minute when Messi fired home from 20 yards – his 12th goal of the tournament. He won Man of the Match, his third trophy and completed a treble of CL Golden Boots!

24

Viktoria Plzen 0 | 4 Barcelona

November, 2011 Messi surpassed 200 goals for Barça in this game, and recorded his second ever hat-trick in the competition too. His third goal was a beauty, with Gerard Pique providing a ridiculous backheeled assist!

GOAL 40
GOAL 41
GOAL 42

GOAL 45
GOAL 46
GOAL 47
GOAL 48
GOAL 49

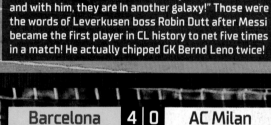

Barcelona 7 | 1 B. Leverkusen

March, 2012 "Without Messi, Barça are the best team, and with him, they are In another galaxy!" Those were the words of Leverkusen boss Robin Dutt after Messi became the first player in CL history to net five times in a match! He actually chipped GK Bernd Leno twice!

GOAL 57
GOAL 58

Barcelona 4 | 0 AC Milan

March, 2013 Wind forward 12 months, and Messi was helping his side make history again! After losing the first leg 2-0, Barça became the first team ever to overturn a two-goal first-leg defeat without the benefit of an away goal – and Leo's sublime brace was a huge help!

Barcelona 4 | 0 Ajax

September, 2013 Ajax were probably cursing their luck when they were drawn in the same group as Barça – and even more so after their Group H opener! Messi scored the fourth Champions League hat-trick of his career, including just his second ever CL free-kick!

GOAL 72
GOAL 73
GOAL 74

GOAL 60
GOAL 61
GOAL 62

APOEL 0 | 4 Barcelona

November, 2014 Records were tumbling for Leo at the end of 2014. He'd just become La Liga's all-time top goalscorer with a hat-trick v Sevilla, and just days later hit a treble against APOEL to break Raul's record of 71 goals to become the CL's all-time top goalscorer too!

GOAL 84
GOAL 85
GOAL 86

GOAL 76
GOAL 77

Barcelona 3 | 0 Bayern Munich

May, 2015 After humiliating Barça 7-0 on aggregate in 2013, it was the German side's defence that were left red-faced in this semi-final! Messi literally sat Jerome Boateng on his bum with a drop of his shoulder, before chipping over Manuel Neuer for his second. World-class!

Barcelona 7 | 0 Celtic

September, 2016 The Scottish side made history at the Nou Camp, but not the kind you want to brag about! Messi's sixth Champions League hat-trick saw The Bhoys suffer their worst ever European defeat. Ouch!

GOAL STATS!

Check out the sick numbers behind Leo's epic 100 Champions League goals...

HOW?
15 Right Foot
4 Header
81 Left Foot

WHEN?
49 First Half
51 Second Half

TYPE?
11 Penalties
3 Free-kicks
86 Open Play

WHERE?
13 Outside Penalty Area
20 Six-yard Box
67 Inside Penalty Area

GOAL 87

GOAL 88

GOAL 89

Barcelona	4	0	Man. City

October, 2016 There was a touch of déjà-vu to this clash, as another quality Messi hat-trick saw a British club leave Spain with their worst ever CL defeat! It took the magician's CL goal tally at the Nou Camp to 50 – overtaking Raul's previous CL home record of 49!

GOAL 94

Barcelona	6	1	PSG

March, 2017 The PSG players tried their best to stop Leo from playing his usual fluid footy, but he still netted from the penalty spot to help his side make history in one of the greatest ever Champo League comebacks!

GOAL 99

GOAL 100

Barcelona	3	0	Chelsea

March, 2018 Messi had finally ended his eight-game drought v Chelsea in the first leg, and he followed it up with two goals through Thibaut Courtois' legs, plus an assist, in the second leg! It was the perfect way to bring up his Champions League ton, as the Barça fans proudly held up a huge 'God Save The King' Messi banner!

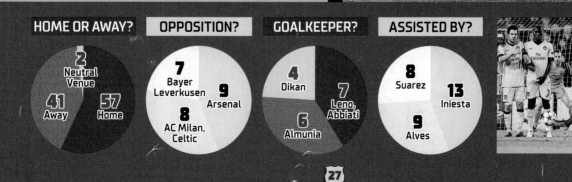

HOME OR AWAY?

2 Neutral Venue
41 Away
57 Home

OPPOSITION?

7 Bayer Leverkusen
9 Arsenal
8 AC Milan, Celtic

GOALKEEPER?

4 Dikan
7 Leno, Abbiati
6 Almunia

ASSISTED BY?

8 Suarez
13 Iniesta
9 Alves

BARÇA S

MATCH has got some inside information you might not already know about your favourite Barcelona heroes!

TER STEGEN

The epic shot stopper played as a striker until he was ten years old, and only started playing in goal because his side's goalkeeper had a nosebleed!

MESSI

A famous Spanish dictionary added a new word in 2013 – which means the perfect way to play football!

inmessionante *adj.* **1.** Calificativo referente a Messi; a su manera perfecta de jugar al fútbol; a su capacidad ilimitada de autosuperación. **2.** Dícese del mejor futbolista de todos los tiempos.

BUSQUETS

The classy central midfielder is the only Blaugrana player without any social media account – no Instagram, Twitter or Facebook!

VIDAL

Arturo really loves horses – he has a horse tattoo on his belly and owns his own stables back in Chile!

ARTHUR

Barça's new No.8's name is easy, right? Wrong! His full name is Arthur Henrique Ramos de Oliveira Melo!

PIQUE

The Barcelona legend uses a WhatsApp group with Real Madrid players to boast about the Catalan club's success. What a wind-up merchant!

TARS revealed!

SUAREZ

The lethal goal king has won over 15 titles, but he's only got one tattooed on his body – the Copa America trophy after Uruguay won it in 2011!

SERGI ROBERTO

The Barça academy boy always packs his Nintendo Switch when they travel to games, and loves beating team-mate Denis Suarez at Mario Kart!

DEMBELE

Dembele's house is just 300 metres from where Neymar used to live and has a cinema room on the third floor. Sweet!

COUTINHO

Philippe has a curved ping-pong table in his back garden, which he uses to play footy tennis. Wicked!

JORDI ALBA

The rapid LB never chooses white pieces when he plays chess, and always likes to brush his teeth before kick-off!

UMTITI

Like Alexis Sanchez, Umtiti's dog is pretty famous on Instagram! The Chow Chow is one of La Liga's most popular pets!

RAKITIC

Ivan is well superstitious! Before every game, he always puts his left sock and left boot on first, but always enters the pitch with his right foot!

29

BARCELONA BRAIN-BUSTER!

How well do you know the Catalan club?

1. What nationality is Barça's awesome box-to-box midfield master Ivan Rakitic?

2. True or False? Barcelona signed Sergi Roberto from Spanish rivals Valencia!

3. Which legend didn't play for Barça – Luis Figo, Ronaldinho or Roberto Carlos?

4. Which Premier League club did ex-Barcelona midfielder Paulinho once play for?

5. For how many years was Pep Guardiola manager of the first team – one, two, three or four?

6. Name the Spain legend who holds the record for most games for the La Liga giants!

7. How old was Lionel Messi when he made his league debut for the senior side?

8. True or False? No team has won the Copa del Rey more times than Barcelona!

9. Who wasn't one of Barça's four captains last season – Messi, Andres Iniesta or Jordi Alba?

10. What year did Uruguay goal machine Luis Suarez join the club – 2013, 2014 or 2015?

1 ....
2 ....
3 ....
4 ....
5 ....
6 ....
7 ....
8 ....
9 ....
10 ....

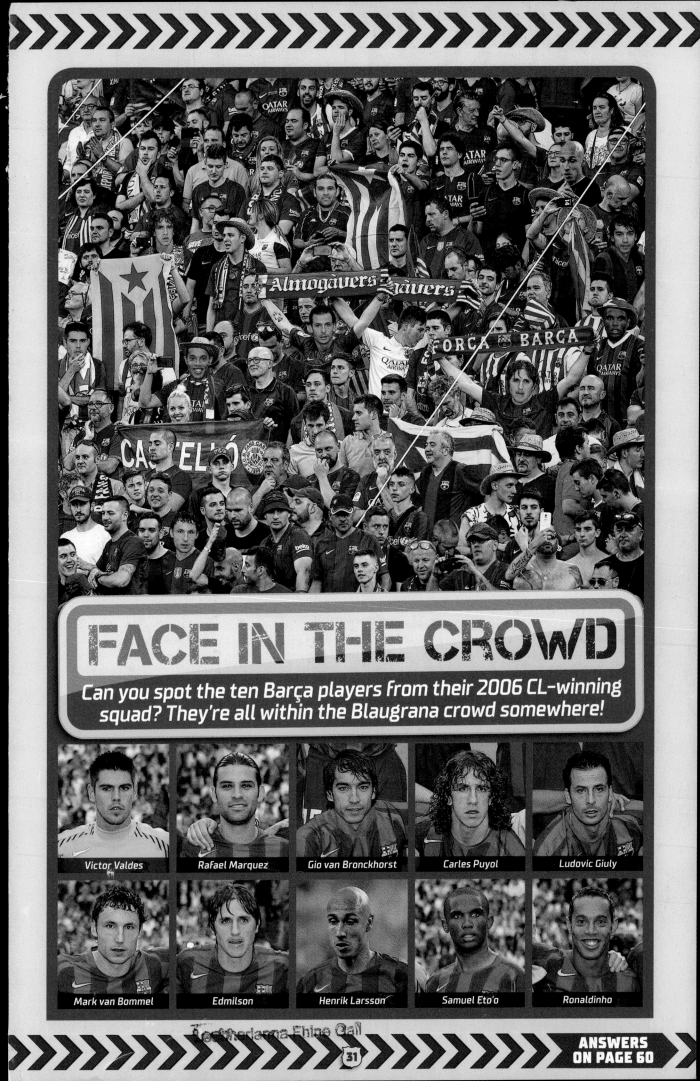

FACE IN THE CROWD

Can you spot the ten Barça players from their 2006 CL-winning squad? They're all within the Blaugrana crowd somewhere!

Victor Valdes

Rafael Marquez

Gio van Bronckhorst

Carles Puyol

Ludovic Giuly

Mark van Bommel

Edmilson

Henrik Larsson

Samuel Eto'o

Ronaldinho

ANSWERS ON PAGE 60

DEMBELE
STAR IN THE MAKING

The lightning-quick wing king is ready to light up the Nou Camp.

Finding a replacement for Neymar in the summer of 2017 – a man that sparkled in the Catalan capital for four seasons – was always going to be tricky. Rumours began, numerous superstars were linked, but the announcement never came. After a few weeks, La Blaugrana fans began to get anxious that they wouldn't find a new attacking hero – especially after seeing their side struggle for inspiration in their two-legged Spanish Super Cup defeat to Real Madrid. But they were eventually rewarded for their patience at the end of August. An exciting, rapid, young forward – tipped to be a future Ballon d'Or winner – was announced for an initial fee of £96.8 million rising to £135.5 million, making him the second-most expensive player ever at the time. That man is now a World Cup winner. That man is Ousmane Dembele...

DORTMUND DIAMOND

You don't just spend close to £100 million on any young player. Barça chiefs had done their homework on Dembele, and after watching him tear it up for Dortmund, they knew he was worth the cash. He averaged more than a goal or assist every other Bundesliga match in 2016-17, while he rocked the Champo League that season, bagging eight goals and assists combined from ten CL games!

THE NEW NEYMAR

The fact almost half the Neymar cash was ploughed back into the Dembele deal suggested Barça saw the France hero as the natural heir to the Brazilian's throne. But when they handed him Neymar's old No.11 shirt, it was obvious! He has similar attributes to his predecessor – mainly his dribbling and tricks. In 2016-17, he completed 103 dribbles in the league – no other Dortmund player reached 60!

HIGH PRAISE

Dembele's 2016-17 displays drew a lot of praise, with many experts in Germany saying he'd challenge for the Ballon d'Or one day. He's had a similar impact on Spanish fans – not least, Xavi. "Dembele's versatile, has many technical and physical qualities, and is very good in the last pass," said the Barça legend to a Spanish newspaper, while Jordi Alba reckons Dembele's even faster than he is!

STOP-START SEASON

Dembele's debut season at Barça didn't go to plan after picking up a serious hamstring injury on his first start. He returned in January, only to suffer another setback. But after working hard to get back, he had a strong end to the season, bagging seven goals and assists combined in his last ten La Liga matches. That included an incredible solo run and chipped goal in the 5-1 win over Villarreal!

FACTPACK

Position: Winger

Country: France

D.O.B: 15/05/1997

Height: 5ft 10in

Boots: Nike Mercurial Vapor

Instagram: o.dembele7

ALL-TIME BARCELONA

DREAM TEAM

Pick your fave XI from Barcelona's best ever players and, if it's the same as MATCH's, you could win an awesome prize!

34

DREAM TEAM
GOALKEEPERS!

CLAUDIO BRAVO
SEASONS: 2014-16

Replacing Victor Valdes was always going to be tricky, but Bravo did a fine job! He didn't concede in the first 754 minutes of his first season, breaking a Spanish league record, and won the Zamora Trophy for the best league goals against average!

ANDONI ZUBIZARRETA
SEASONS: 1986-94

When Zubi signed in 1986 for €1.7 million, he became the most expensive GK in the world at the time. He ended up being value for money though, captaining the side for five seasons and leading them to European Cup glory in 1992!

JAVIER URRUTICOECHEA
SEASONS: 1981-88

Urruti won the Zamora Trophy in 1983-84, and secured his status as one of the club's greatest ever goalkeepers – and a total Barcelona legend – in 1985, when his penalty save against Valladolid virtually sealed the La Liga title. Hero!

VICTOR VALDES
SEASONS: 2002-14

Valdes progressed through the Barça academy, and eventually left as the most decorated GK in the club's history with 21 major trophies! He's also the only keeper to feature in Barça's all-time top ten list of appearance makers!

MARC-ANDRE TER STEGEN
SEASONS: 2014-PRESENT

It might have taken Ter Stegen some time to establish himself as the club's No.1, but he's proven his worth since! His shot-stopping last season was incredible, and some footy experts reckon he's become the best keeper on the planet!

BEST OF THE REST...   CHECK OUT THESE OTHER SUPERSTARS!

RUUD HESP
Seasons: 1997-2000

SALVADOR SADURNI
Seasons: 1960-76

VITOR BAIA
Seasons: 1996-98

ANTONI RAMALLETS
Seasons: 1946-62

NOW PICK YOUR ALL-TIME BARCELONA DREAM TEAM GOALKEEPER!

TURN TO PAGE 42

DREAM TEAM
FULL-BACKS!

GIANLUCA ZAMBROTTA

SEASONS: 2006-08

The slick Italy right-back joined Barça off the back of winning the World Cup, so the Catalan club knew they were getting a top player. He played 58 league games for them and was a solid addition to the side, even if it was just for a brief spell!

SERGI BARJUAN

SEASONS: 1993-2002

If you watched videos of Sergi, you'd probably think you were watching retro clips of Jordi Alba! The left-back came through the ranks at Barça, and was best known for his powerful, attacking runs and threat going forward!

JORDI ALBA

SEASONS: 2012-PRESENT

The wicked Spain left-back flies up and down the flank all game – at a lightning-quick speed! He was a bit of an assist king last season too, setting up eight La Liga goals for his team-mates – more than any Barça or Real Madrid midfielder!

GIOVANNI VAN BRONCKHORST

SEASONS: 2003-07

After impressing on loan from Arsenal, Barcelona decided to sign Gio permanently! The midfielder-turned classy left-back helped the Spanish giants to league glory in 2004-05, and then to a league and CL double the year after!

DANI ALVES

SEASONS: 2008-16

Rampaging runs, outrageous touches and a great understanding with Messi – Alves was a real crowd pleaser during his time at Barça! The fact he won six La Liga titles, four Copa del Rey medals and three Champo Leagues wasn't bad either!

BEST OF THE REST... CHECK OUT THESE OTHER SUPERSTARS!

LILIAN THURAM
Seasons: 2006-08

ERIC ABIDAL
Seasons: 2007-13

ALBERT FERRER
Seasons: 1990-98

MICHAEL REIZIGER
Seasons: 1997-2004

NOW PICK YOUR ALL-TIME BARCELONA DREAM TEAM FULL-BACKS!

TURN TO PAGE 42

RAFAEL MARQUEZ

SEASONS: 2003-10

Mexico legend Marquez was class as a CB and at DM, which made him a key man for the club. He ended his seven-year spell as the most-capped non-European player in Barça's history – and with four La Ligas and a CL title in the bag!

JAVIER MASCHERANO

SEASONS: 2010-18

Masch started his Barça career playing out of position as a CB – or that's what everyone thought! He ended up nailing down a starting place alongside Pique in the Barça defence, and looked just as good there as he ever did at DM!

RONALD KOEMAN

SEASONS: 1989-95

The Dutchman helped Barça win four La Ligas in a row between 1991 and 1994, and netted the winner in the European Cup final in 1992! His scoring record was outrageous for a CB – averaging better than a goal every three games in all comps!

GERARD PIQUE

SEASONS: 2008-PRESENT

Pique left La Masia to join Man. United on a free transfer in 2004, but was re-signed by La Blaugrana in 2008. He's clearly got Barça DNA – his classiness on the ball and ability to play out from the back is second to none!

CARLES PUYOL

SEASONS: 1999-2014

Puyol was one of the best defenders the planet has ever seen! He was a fans' favourite for his strong tackling and body-on-the-line commitment, and the fact he spent his entire career with Los Cules makes him a total legend!

BEST OF THE REST... CHECK OUT THESE OTHER SUPERSTARS!

SAMUEL UMTITI
Seasons: 2016-Present

MIGUELI
Seasons: 1973-88

GHEORGHE POPESCU
Seasons: 1995-97

JOSE RAMON ALEXANCO
Seasons: 1980-93

NOW PICK YOUR ALL-TIME BARCELONA DREAM TEAM CENTRE-BACKS!

TURN TO PAGE 42

DREAM TEAM
MIDFIELDERS!

DECO
SEASONS: 2004-08

If you want some flair in midfield, look no further than Deco! The Portugal baller, who was born and raised in Brazil, was all about making footy fun to watch! He knew all the tricks in the book, and could get himself out of any situation!

ANDRES INIESTA
SEASONS: 2002-18

You just had to watch Iniesta's farewell ceremony at the end of 2017-18 to see how much he meant to Barça! The incredibly technical playmaker won every trophy on offer during his career, and wowed fans with his amazing ball control!

JOHAN CRUYFF
SEASONS: 1973-78

Cruyff became the most expensive player in the world when he joined Barça in 1973, and helped them win La Liga for the first time in 13 years! He won two Ballons d'Or while he was at the club, and is still seen as one of their greatest ever icons!

SERGIO BUSQUETS
SEASONS: 2008-PRESENT

Busquets isn't your average DM, in that he isn't known for his tough tackling or energetic displays. But he's perfect for Barça – he sits in front of the two centre-backs and dictates the game at the pace he wants it to be played at!

LUIS ENRIQUE
SEASONS: 1996-2004

Fans were unsure of Enrique when he joined from Real Madrid on a free transfer, but he soon won over Los Cules' hearts – especially after scoring in El Clasico! He eventually became captain, and was known for his energy and versatility!

BEST OF THE REST... CHECK OUT THESE OTHER SUPERSTARS!

PHILLIP COCU
Seasons: 1998-2004

THIAGO MOTTA
Seasons: 2001-07

YAYA TOURE
Seasons: 2007-10

JOSE MARI BAKERO
Seasons: 1988-96

SEYDOU KEITA
Seasons: 2008-12

PEP GUARDIOLA

SEASONS: 1990-2001

Pep had a similar style of play to Xavi – he was the team's organiser in midfield, controlling matches with his positioning, passing and understanding of the game. He won six La Liga titles during his Barça career, plus the European Cup!

XAVI

SEASONS: 1998-2015

Xavi is living proof that you don't have to be big and strong to boss a midfield! He was such an intelligent player, and had the passing ability to match his epic vision. He always wanted the ball, and always knew where it should go next. Legend!

JOHAN NEESKENS

SEASONS: 1974-79

Neeskens was called Johan II after joining from Ajax to partner his old team-mate Cruyff, but he was a different player with more physical presence in midfield. He was so popular that even after he left the club, fans would still sing his name!

BERND SCHUSTER

SEASONS: 1980-88

Schuster was Barça's driving force in the 1980s, and even though he wasn't club captain, he was always one of the first players to motivate his side when things weren't going to plan. He was technically special, too – especially from set-pieces!

IVAN RAKITIC

SEASONS: 2014-PRESENT

In his first season at the club, Barça achieved an historic treble – the classy Croatian had only won two trophies in his entire career before then! His tally for Barça is now at 11, and his importance to the team has grown and grown over the years!

BEST OF THE REST... CHECK OUT THESE OTHER SUPERSTARS!

GHEORGHE HAGI

Seasons: 1994-96

EDMILSON

Seasons: 2004-08

GUILLERMO AMOR

Seasons: 1988-98

JUAN ROMAN RIQUELME

Seasons: 2002-05

NOW PICK YOUR ALL-TIME BARCELONA DREAM TEAM MIDFIELDERS!

TURN TO PAGE 42

DREAM TEAM
FORWARDS!

RONALDINHO
SEASONS: 2003-08

Ronaldinho is the definition of footy flair! He'd have fans on their feet with his epic tekkers – including once at the Bernabeu in 2005! He left with two La Ligas, a Champions League crown and, most importantly, as a Ballon d'Or winner. Legend!

RONALDO
SEASONS: 1996-97

Even though he went on to star for Real Madrid, Ronaldo made such an impact in his only season with Los Cules. After joining aged 20, he scored an incredible 47 goals in 49 games for Barça in all competitions – a record that is just ridiculous!

SAMUEL ETO'O
SEASONS: 2004-09

For five years, Cameroon icon Eto'o was Barcelona's main man up top! He was an absolutely deadly goalscorer, netting 130 times in 199 games, in both the 2006 and 2009 CL finals, and finishing as La Liga top scorer on two occasions!

RIVALDO
SEASONS: 1997-2002

Another of Barça's Brazilian Ballon d'Or winners, Rivaldo was mega skilful and had a rocket left foot! Make sure you YouTube his mind-boggling overhead kick against Valencia – it's one of the best goals MATCH has ever seen!

ROMARIO
SEASONS: 1993-95

In his first season at the Nou Camp, Romario busted 30 nets in just 33 La Liga matches! Ex-Real Madrid gaffer Jorge Valdano described him as a 'comic book player', because his demon dribbling, searing pace and lethal finishing just didn't seem real!

BEST OF THE REST...   CHECK OUT THESE OTHER SUPERSTARS!

PATRICK KLUIVERT
Seasons: 1998-2004

HENRIK LARSSON
Seasons: 2004-06

GARY LINEKER
Seasons: 1986-89

MARC OVERMARS
Seasons: 2000-04

DAVID VILLA
Seasons: 2010-13

NEYMAR

SEASONS: 2013-17

Loads of fans still can't forgive Neymar for leaving, but the impact he had at the club was outstanding. On top of all his tricks, assists and goals, they can't forget his display against PSG in the 2016-17 CL, when they made history at the Nou Camp!

PEDRO

SEASONS: 2008-15

Pedro broke into the starting XI in 2009, before becoming a regular! He won 20 trophies and became a world-record breaker in 2009-10 – becoming the first footballer ever to score in six different club competitions in one season!

LIONEL MESSI

SEASONS: 2004-PRESENT

A strong candidate for the best player ever, Messi has broken so many records at Barcelona! But with five Ballons d'Or, and more than double the number of goals than any other Barça player, Leo will forever be a club legend!

DIEGO MARADONA

SEASONS: 1982-84

Many experts' G.O.A.T, Maradona spent two seasons at Barça – not long enough for La Blaugrana fans! His dribbling skills and agility were out of this world, and he was another of the very few opponents to get clapped for a goal at the Bernabeu!

LUIS SUAREZ

SEASONS: 2014-PRESENT

Suarez's stats are savage – he hit 110 goals in his first 130 La Liga games! An epic 40 of those came in the 2015-16 season, where he also bagged 16 assists, becoming the first player ever to top the La Liga goals and assist charts. Hero!

BEST OF THE REST... CHECK OUT THESE OTHER SUPERSTARS!

MICHAEL LAUDRUP
Seasons: 1989-94

THIERRY HENRY
Seasons: 2007-10

HRISTO STOICHKOV
Seasons: 1990-95 & 96-98

ZLATAN IBRAHIMOVIC
Seasons: 2009-11

NOW PICK YOUR ALL-TIME BARCELONA DREAM TEAM FORWARDS!

DREAM TEAM
MY ALL-TIME BARÇA XI!

You've seen MATCH's all-time Barça shortlist, now pick your fave starting XI!

GOALKEEPER

RIGHT-BACK

CENTRE-BACK

CENTRE-BACK

LEFT-BACK

MIDFIELDER

MIDFIELDER

MIDFIELDER

FORWARD

FORWARD

FORWARD

WIN! A BARÇA 2018-19 KIDS HOME SHIRT!

SPORTS DIRECT

Pick your favourite team and if it's the same as MATCH's all-time Barcelona XI, you'll be put into the draw! One lucky reader will then be picked at random to win a 2018-19 Barcelona kids home shirt, thanks to our top mates at Sports Direct. Get entering now!

Just Fill in your Dream Team and details, then send a photocopy of this page to: Barcelona Dream Team 2019, MATCH Magazine, Kelsey Media, Regent House, Welbeck Way, Peterborough, Cambridgeshire, PE2 7WH

Closing date: January 31, 2019.

Name:

Date of birth:

Address:

Mobile:

Email:

Kids shirt size:

CALL YOURSELF A CULE?

MATCH takes a look at what it really means to be a Barça supporter!

Barça fans call themselves 'Los Cules', which actually means 'The Bums!' It dates back to the 1920s when supporters would sit on walls around the stadium to watch the games – and people walking in the street could see their bottoms from below!

Barça's motto is 'Mes que un club' – 'More than a club' in English – and can be seen on the seats at the Nou Camp!

CULE CHECKLIST

See how many of these you can tick off!

Get snapped in a Barcelona shirt!

Take a tour of the Nou Camp's museum!

Watch the stars arrive for a game in their cars!

Cheer them on at a match in the Nou Camp!

Follow all the players on Instagram!

Stick a Barça hero MATCH poster on your wall!

Practise and perfect the Cruyff turn!

Beat Real Madrid 5-0 in a friendly on FIFA!

Learn the tune to the Barça hymn – see right!

CANT DEL BARÇA

You must have heard Barça's famous hymn – it rings around the Nou Camp before and after every home match!

The whole stadium,
Cheers loudly,
We're the blue and maroon supporters,
No matter where we come from,
Be it south or north,
Now we all agree – we all agree,
One flag unites us as brothers.

Blue maroon in the wind,
A valiant cry,
We have a name everyone knows,
Barça, Barça, Baaarça!

Players, Supporters,
United we are strong,
Many years full of support.

We have cheered many goals,
And we have shown – we have shown,
That no-one can ever break us.

Blue maroon in the wind,
A valiant cry,
We have a name everyone knows,
Barça, Barça, Baaarça!

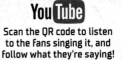

Scan the QR code to listen to the fans singing it, and follow what they're saying!

43

STAT ATTACK!

Get a load of BARÇA's biggest signings, mega trophy cabinet, record goalscorers, Ballon d'Or winners and tons more!

FIVE BIGGEST SIGNINGS

	PLAYER	YEAR	FEE
1	Philippe Coutinho	2018	£142m
2	Ousmane Dembele	2017	£135.5m
3	Luis Suarez	2014	£65m
4	Zlatan Ibrahimovic	2009	£57m
5	Neymar	2013	£48.6m

FIVE BIGGEST SALES

	PLAYER	YEAR	FEE
1	Neymar	2017	£198m
2	Luis Figo	2000	£37.2m
3	Alexis Sanchez	2014	£35m
4	Cesc Fabregas	2014	£27m
5	Yaya Toure	2010	£24m

MAJOR TROPHIES

- **5** Champions League
- **3** FIFA Club World Cup
- **4** European Cup Winners' Cup
- **3** Fairs Cup
- **5** European Super Cup
- **25** La Liga
- **30** Copa del Rey
- **12** Spanish Super Cup

MOST APPEARANCES

Player		Appearances
Xavi	1998–2015	767
Andres Iniesta	2002–2018	674
Lionel Messi	2004–	637
Carles Puyol	1999–2014	593
Migueli	1973–1989	549
Victor Valdes	2002–2014	535
Sergio Busquets	2008–	482
Carlos Rexach	1965–1981	449
Gerard Pique	2008–	446
Guillermo Amor	1988–1998	421

Legendary playmaker Andres Iniesta is the only Barcelona star to have won four Champions League medals and played in all four of those finals!

CHAMPIONS LEAGUE RECORD
ALL-TIME

PLAYED	WON
236	**138**

LOST	DRAWN
42	**56**

GOALS	CONCEDED
476	**231**

17 There were a massive 17 points separating Barcelona and Real Madrid in 2017-18 – the biggest gap between the two teams in a decade!

ALL-TIME TOP SCORERS

- Lionel Messi **552**
- Cesar **232**
- Laszlo Kubala **194**
- Josep Samitier **184**
- Josep Escola **167**
- Luis Suarez **152**
- Paulino Alcantara **143**
- Angel Arocha **134**
- Samuel Eto'o **130**
- Rivaldo **130**

91 Lionel Messi scored a gigantic 91 goals in 2012 – the most nets ever busted by a player in a calendar year. Wow!

11 Number of Barcelona Ballon d'Or winners!

- Luis Suarez 1960
- Johan Cruyff 1973 & 1974
- Hristo Stoichkov 1994
- Rivaldo 1999
- Ronaldinho 2005
- Lionel Messi 2009, 2010, 2011, 2012 & 2015

BIGGEST VICTORIES

LA LIGA HOME
10-1
v Gimnastic de Tarragona, 1949

LA LIGA AWAY
0-8
v Deportivo, 2016*

*Also beat three other teams 8-0

facebook 103+ MILLION Likes

Instagram 57+ MILLION Likes

twitter 29+ MILLION Likes

Stats only include official matches. Correct up to start of the 2018-19 season.

BARÇA'S RECORD BREAKERS!

Meet the men who've broken awesome records at the Nou Camp!

VICTOR VALDES

Valdes won his fifth Zamora Trophy – the goalkeeper award for lowest goals-to-game ratio – in 2011-12, equalling ex-Barcelona keeper Antoni Ramallets' record!

Zamora Trophies	5
Consecutive Zamora Trophies	4

ANDONI ZUBIZARRETA

The record appearance maker in Spanish footy history made over 300 of his league appearances for Barcelona – more than for any other side during his career!

La Liga games	622
La Liga clean sheets	233
Copa del Rey games	104

XAVI

The world-class playmaker was known for his accurate passing, and in their 2013 Champo League clash against PSG he made and completed all 96 of his passes!

First footballer to play 150 CL matches	150
CL passes with a 100% record	96
Passes in a European Championship game	136

ANDRES INIESTA

Iniesta is undoubtedly one of the greatest midfielders ever – and his trophy collection is proof of that!

Spanish player with most trophies	35
La Liga unbeaten streak	55

LASZLO KUBALA

The Hungarian forward was such a legendary player at Barcelona in the 1950s that he even has his own statue outside the Nou Camp!

La Liga goals in one match	7

SERGIO BUSQUETS

Busquets has always been a bit of an unsung hero at Barça, but the way he keeps the ball and games ticking over helps the team win!

Consecutive La Liga wins	25

LIONEL MESSI

It seems like a month never goes by without Leo Messi breaking or making records!

Club & country goals in a calendar year	91	La Liga assists	149
Club goals in a calendar year	79	La Liga-game scoring streak	21
Champions League hat-tricks	7	European Golden Shoes	5
La Liga goals	383	Ballon d'Or awards	5

TRANSFER RECORD BREAKERS!

Barcelona have been involved in loads of world-record deals – both in and out!

1982
Diego Maradona

from Boca Juniors
£3 million

1996
Ronaldo

From PSV
£13.2 million

1997
Ronaldo

to Inter
£19.5 million

2000
Luis Figo

to Real Madrid
£37.2 million

2017
Neymar

to PSG
£198 million

CROSSWORD

Use the clues to fill in this awesome Barça crossword puzzle!

ACROSS

5. Barcelona's second highest La Liga goalscorer in the 2017-18 season! [4,6]

8. Team that knocked them out of the CL in 2017-18! [4]

9. Shirt number of classy defender Gerard Pique! [5]

12. Team that ended Barça's awesome unbeaten La Liga run in May 2018! [7]

14. Bonkers nickname of Lionel Messi, The _ _ _ _! [4]

15. Legendary Portugal ace that played for Barcelona and Real Madrid! [4,4]

17. Name of Barça's famous youth academy! [2,5]

19. Swiss team midfielder Ivan Rakitic started his epic career with! [5]

DOWN

1. Name of the Catalan club's big city rivals! [8]

2. Country that legendary striker Hristo Stoichkov used to play for! [8]

3. One of the club's awesome nicknames! [3,5]

4. Quality Barcelona legend, Xavi _ _ _ _ _ _ _ _ _! [9]

6. Surname of the Barça hero on the cover of Pro Evolution Soccer 2019! [8]

7. Number of Colombian players in their first-team squad in 2017-18! [3]

10. Shirt number Andres Iniesta used to wear! [5]

11. Country that wicked playmaker Philippe Coutinho plays for! [6]

13. Name of Barcelona's huge iconic stadium! [3,4]

14. Number of Champions League titles the Spanish giants have won! [4]

16. Successful ex-gaffer Rijkaard's first name! [5]

18. Mega boot brand Barça heroes Lionel Messi and Jordi Alba both wear! [6]

NAME THE TEAM

The stars from Barcelona's 2017-18 Champo League clash with Chelsea at the Nou Camp are hidden – work out who they are!

1. Goalkeeper

2. Centre-back

3. Midfielder

4. Defensive midfielder

5. Centre-back

6. Forward

7. Right-back

8. Forward

9. Midfielder

10. Striker

11. Left-back

ANSWERS ON PAGE 60

ANDRES INIESTA'S...
BARCELONA

JOINS LA MASIA
September 1996
After impressing for his local town's team Albacete, Iniesta was invited to join Barcelona's academy La Masia! He was a shy 12-year-old boy, and cried for days when he first left his parents, but it all turned out pretty well in the end!

BARCELONA DEBUT
October 2002
Iniesta made a name for himself in the youth teams, and was eventually handed his senior debut in a Champo League match v Club Brugge! Even today, the legendary playmaker says it was the most important moment of his career!

HELPS SECURE DOUBLE
May 2006
After helping Barça win back-to-back La Ligas, he was left on the bench for the 2006 CL final v Arsenal. Los Cules were 1-0 down when he came on at half-time, but his display helped his side win 2-1 – and saw him lift his first CL trophy!

CHELSEA WORLDY
May 2009
Maybe the most iconic moment of Iniesta's Barcelona career was his epic last-gasp goal against Chelsea in the semi-final of the 2009 Champions League! It was such a sweet strike, and he then put on a quality show in the final v Man. United to seal his second CL title!

Scrapbook!

He might have left the Catalan club, but Iniesta will always be remembered as a Barça legend! Check out his career in pics...

NATIONAL HERO
July 2010
Scoring Spain's winning goal in the 2010 World Cup final turned him into a national hero! In the 2010-11 season, he was applauded off at every ground, including city rivals Espanyol in December 2010!

BALLON D'OR RUNNER-UP
January 2011
In an all-Barça final three, Iniesta came second only to Leo Messi for the 2010 Ballon d'Or! Xavi grabbed the final place on the podium, but it was the closest Andres came to being named the best player in the world!

BECOMES CAPTAIN

August 2015

When the legendary Xavi left the club in the summer of 2015, the Barcelona armband was up for grabs! The players voted for who they wanted to lead them, and Andres was chosen as their man!

CHAMPO LEAGUE MASTERCLASS

June 2015

It was Andres' assist to Ivan Rakitic which gave Barcelona the breakthrough in their 2015 CL final win over Juventus! He went on to totally dominate the game and win UEFA's Man of the Match award!

OVATION AT THE BERNABEU

November 2015

In his first Clasico as leader of La Blaugrana, he didn't disappoint! He put on such a sublime showing in a 4-0 win, he was even clapped off by the Real Madrid fans when he was substituted – and that doesn't happen very often!

HISTORY MAKER

May 2017

Barcelona's 3-1 win over Alaves in the 2017 Copa del Rey was Iniesta's 33rd trophy of his career – meaning he overtook Xavi as the most decorated player in Spanish footy history!

INIESTA'S FINAL

April 2018

The 2018 Copa del Rey final v Sevilla was later to be known as 'The Iniesta Final' after the legend's mind-blowing performance and stunning goal! It turned out to be the last trophy he'd lift as Barça captain, but he'd saved the best till last!

ADIOS ANDRES

April 2018

In an emotional press conference, Iniesta announced he'd be leaving the club he'd spent 22 years at! Soon after, Barcelona and Nike released a special edition 'Infinite Iniesta' shirt to mark his legendary status at the club!

THE END

May 2018

His last ever game in a Barcelona shirt came against Real Sociedad. With a guard of honour, a jaw-dropping mosaic and fans chanting his name, it was a special end to the playmaker's incredible Barça career!

TOP 5...
BARÇA RIVALS!

The La Liga super club have made some massive footy enemies over the years! Here we count down their top five rivals...

5 MAN. UNITED

This rivalry was born in the Champions League between 1990 and 2000, when the mega clubs met four times – and once in the European Cup Winners' Cup. The Catalans have the upper hand in the most important meetings though, beating The Red Devils in both the 2009 and 2011 CL finals!

HEAD-TO-HEAD

Barça Wins	4	Draws	4	United Wins	3

VILLAIN
PAUL SCHOLES

Having fallen behind Real Madrid in the 2007–08 La Liga season, and being knocked out in the semi-final of the Copa del Rey, the CL was Barcelona's last shot at a trophy. They met United in the semis, only for Scholes to knock them out!

HERO
XAVI

The legendary playmaker had a blinder when the two met in the 2009 CL final, winning UEFA's Man of the Match and securing the club's historic treble! He then dominated the midfield again in the 2011 final, with Barça running out 3-1 winners!

4 ATHLETIC BILBAO

Barça and Athletic are the Copa del Rey kings, sitting first and second respectively on the list of cup wins. But their tense rivalry isn't just down to wanting to out-title each other. In the 1984 final, Bilbao won 1-0 and a big brawl broke out between the two sets of players – and it's never been forgotten!

HEAD-TO-HEAD

Barça Wins	113	Draws	36	Athletic Wins	74

VILLAIN
ANDONI GOIKOETXEA

The no-nonsense CB was known as the 'Butcher from Bilbao' for his tough tackling! He became one of Barcelona's biggest villains after he badly injured star player Bernd Schuster in 1981, before doing the same to Diego Maradona in 1983!

HERO
LUIS FIGO

Not many Barça fans could ever accept Luis Figo as a hero after he joined rivals Real Madrid in 2000, but it was his double in the 1997 Copa del Rey Final that saw Los Cules join Bilbao as the most successful club ever in the famous tournament!

3 CHELSEA

Chelsea and Barcelona have one of the greatest European rivalries, formed after some massive Champions League battles! They've met 14 times since the turn of the century – most recently in last season's Round of 16 – and there's been plenty of late drama, controversy and stunning goals!

HEAD-TO-HEAD

Barça Wins	6	Draws	6	Chelsea Wins	5

VILLAIN
FERNANDO TORRES

Chelsea got revenge for a semi-final exit to Barça three years earlier by scraping through the 2012 semi at the Nou Camp. John Terry got sent off in the first half, but Torres popped up with a 90th-minute equaliser – sending The Blues through!

HERO
ANDRES INIESTA

After a goalless first leg in the 2008-09 semi-final, Michael Essien gave Chelsea a lead in the return at Stamford Bridge! However, Iniesta hit an absolute bullet into the net in added time to send La Blaugrana into the final on away goals!

2 ESPANYOL

The 'Derbi Barceloni' pits the two big city rivals together, and although the head-to-head is pretty one-sided, there's always an edge to the game. The RCDE Stadium, just three miles from the Nou Camp, is probably the one place in the city that you'll hear people speak badly about the likes of Messi and co!

HEAD-TO-HEAD

Barça Wins	121	Draws	43	Espanyol Wins	44

VILLAIN
IVAN DE LA PENA

He came through the Barcelona academy and played over 100 games, but joined city rivals Espanyol in 2002. As if that wasn't bad enough, he then hit a brace at the Nou Camp in 2009 to help Espanyol to their first win there for 27 years!

HERO
GERARD PIQUE

Espanyol probably see Pique as their biggest villain, but the CB silenced their fans in February 2018. Barça were losing 1-0 at RCDE, and in danger of missing out on a record unbeaten start to a season, but Pique headed in a quality late equaliser!

1 REAL MADRID

Of course El Clasico is 'numero uno'! Millions of fans from all over the world tune in to watch Spain's two super clubs battle it out, and it rarely disappoints. Not only does it boast some of the best players on the planet, there's also so much history between the Spanish giants, which creates extra tension!

HEAD-TO-HEAD

Barça Wins	92	Draws	50	Real Wins	95

VILLAIN
JOSE MOURINHO

The outspoken gaffer, who was an interpreter at Barcelona in the early 90s, is the man every Barça fan loves to hate! The rivalry started when he was in charge of Chelsea, but then got really out of hand during his three-year stint as Real boss!

HERO
LIONEL MESSI

With 26 Clasico goals, eight more than any other player, Leo is El Clasico's king! His display in April 2017 at the Bernabeu – netting a last-gasp winner with his 500th goal for Barça – could be the best individual Clasico performance ever!

UMTITI
FUTURE LEADER

The World Cup winner's new deal showed his commitment to Barça.

Top-quality players are like magnets to transfer gossip – just ask Samuel Umtiti. Man. United, Man. City and PSG were just a few of the European giants linked with the France defender in the 2018 January transfer window. With a release clause in his contract of £53 million – a really low fee given his huge potential, plus the fact that Liverpool had just forked out £75 million on Virgil van Dijk to shatter the world transfer record for a defender – it was normal that rival clubs were tempted to activate it. It didn't take Barça's bosses long to realise they had to stop clubs from sniffing around Umtiti – but first they had to convince him to stay. Luckily for them, the centre-back always saw his future with the club, and after some negotiating, he penned a new deal to stay in the Catalan capital for the foreseeable future...

MEGA RELEASE CLAUSE

June 4, 2018 will always be a day to remember for Umtiti – and for fans of La Blaugrana. It was the day the France CB agreed a new five-year deal with Barça – and the day his release clause was almost multiplied by nine! Any club that wants to sign Umtiti should start saving now, because his buy-out fee has risen to £437 million! That means only an astronomical offer can take him away from the Nou Camp!

DEFENSIVE KING

Barça have always had commanding CBs at the heart of their defence – from Koeman to Puyol, Pique to... Umtiti! With Pique now in his early 30s, Cameroon-born Umtiti is the natural replacement to take over from him once he retires. His aim will be to learn as much from the Spain centre-back as possible, and be as prepared as he can to lead and boss the backline when the time comes.

MALDINI MODEL

One of Umtiti's footy idols growing up was Paolo Maldini. The legendary AC Milan and Italy defender was known for his technique, athleticism and composure – all attributes that Umtiti has shown he possesses big-time since joining Barcelona in 2016. Just like Maldini, he loves receiving the ball from the goalkeeper, moving up the field and seeking out a team-mate with an accurate forward pass.

MAKING HISTORY

Barça let in just 29 goals last term – the second lowest in the league – and five of those came from the final match week when Umtiti wasn't playing! They actually set a new club record at the start of the season too, conceding just four goals in their opening 12 La Liga games. They were just one goal from equalling the La Liga record – Atletico conceded only three from 12 at the start of 1995-96.

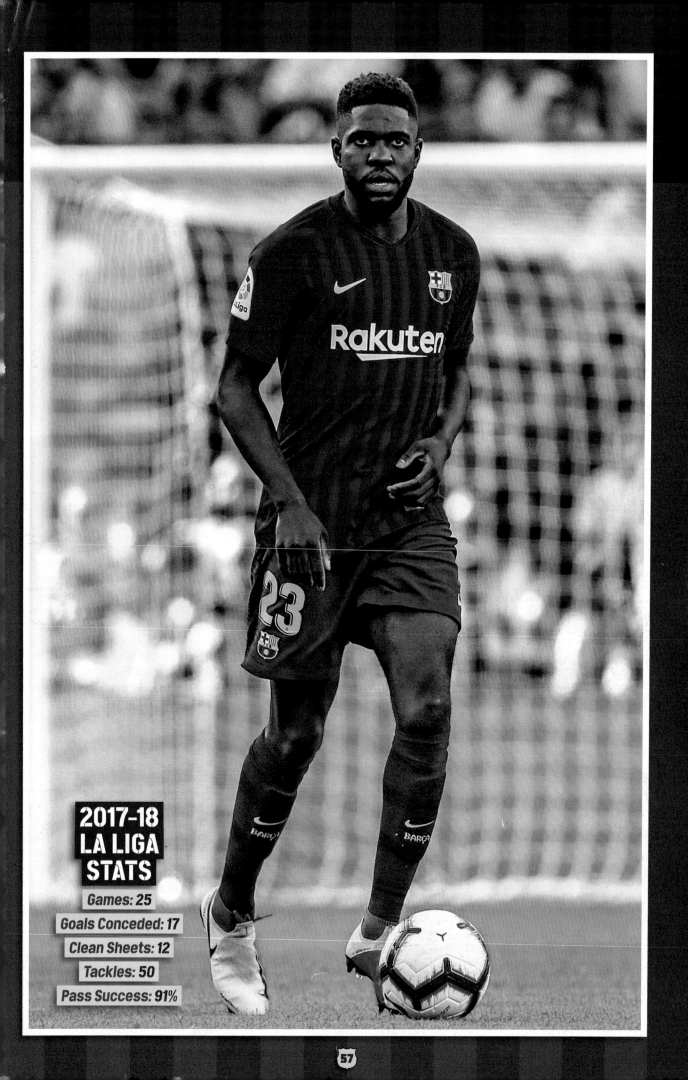

2017-18 LA LIGA STATS

Games: 25

Goals Conceded: 17

Clean Sheets: 12

Tackles: 50

Pass Success: 91%

2018-19 FIRST TEAM SQUAD

GOALKEEPERS

No.	Player		La Liga Games/Goals 2017-18	Signed from
1	Marc-A. ter Stegen		37/0	B. M'gladbach, 2014
13	Jasper Cillessen		1/0	Ajax, 2016

Cillessen

DEFENDERS

No.	Player		La Liga Games/Goals 2017-18	Signed from
2	Nelson Semedo		24/0	Benfica, 2017
3	Gerard Pique		30/2	Man. United, 2008
15	Clement Lenglet		35/3	Sevilla, 2018
18	Jordi Alba		33/2	Valencia, 2012
23	Samuel Umtiti		25/1	Lyon, 2016
24	Thomas Vermaelen		14/0	Arsenal, 2014

Rakuten

beko

Gillette

KONAMI

MÉS QUE UN CLUB

Lenglet

MIDFIELDERS

No.	Player		La Liga Games/Goals 2017-18	Signed from
4	Ivan Rakitic		35/1	Sevilla, 2014
5	Sergio Busquets		31/1	Academy
6	Denis Suarez		18/2	Villarreal, 2016
7	Philippe Coutinho		18/8	Liverpool, 2018
8	Arthur		N/A	Gremio, 2018
12	Rafinha		N/A	Academy
16	Sergi Samper		2/0	Academy
20	Sergi Roberto		30/1	Academy
22	Arturo Vidal		N/A	Bayern Munich, 2018
–	Carlos Alena		0/0	Academy

C B

Malcom

FORWARDS

No.	Player		La Liga Games/Goals 2017-18	Signed from
9	Luis Suarez		33/25	Liverpool, 2014
10	Lionel Messi		36/34	Academy
11	Ousmane Dembele		17/3	B. Dortmund, 2017
14	Malcom		N/A	Bordeaux, 2018
19	Munir		33/10	Academy

MEET THE MANAGER...

ERNESTO VALVERDE

Country: Spain

D.O.B: 9 February, 1964

Former Club: Athletic Bilbao

**Honours: 1x La Liga,
1x Copa del Rey,
1x Spanish Super Cup,
3x Greece Super League**

After winning his first ever La Liga title on his first attempt as Barcelona manager, Valverde played down his own role in the success. "I tried to fit into the team's dynamic and, sometimes, just not get in the way too much." It was a cheeky comment, but one which says a lot about the brilliant boss' coaching style.

The ex-Blaugrana striker isn't desperate to be the centre of attention, play ridiculous managerial mind games or force his players to respect him. The quiet conductor quite simply doesn't need to – his squad of stars show their commitment and desire with their quality performances on the pitch.

After getting thrashed 5-1 on aggregate in the Spanish Super Cup by Real Madrid in August 2017, fans feared the worst for the new season. But it wasn't long before Valverde had the side playing to his organised, effective style, and the records soon started to tumble in what was quite an incredible first year in charge – almost going the entire La Liga season unbeaten!

QUIZ ANSWERS ►►►►►►►►►►►►►

Wordsearch P16

Brain-Buster P30

1. Croatian
2. False
3. Roberto Carlos
4. Tottenham
5. Four
6. Xavi
7. 17 years old
8. True
9. Jordi Alba
10. 2014

Name The Team P49

1. Marc-Andre ter Stegen
2. Samuel Umtiti
3. Ivan Rakitic
4. Sergio Busquets
5. Gerard Pique
6. Lionel Messi
7. Sergi Roberto
8. Ousmane Dembele
9. Andres Iniesta
10. Luis Suarez
11. Jordi Alba

Spot The Difference P17

Crossword P48

Face In The Crowd P31

60

LOVE MATCH?
GET IT DELIVERED EVERY WEEK!

PACKED EVERY WEEK WITH...

- ★ Red-hot gear
- ★ FIFA tips
- ★ Stats & quizzes
- ★ Massive stars
- ★ Posters & pics
- & loads more!

4 ISSUES FOR JUST £1!*

ROLL OF HONOUR

CHAMPIONS LEAGUE
1991-92, 2005-06, 2008-09, 2010-11, 2014-15

FIFA CLUB WORLD CUP
2009, 2011, 2015

EUROPEAN CUP WINNERS' CUP
1978-79, 1981-82, 1988-89, 1996-97

FAIRS CUP
1957-58, 1959-60, 1965-66 (won outright in 1971)

EUROPEAN SUPER CUP
1992, 1997, 2009, 2011, 2015

LA LIGA
1928-29, 1944-45, 1947-48, 1948-49, 1951-52, 1952-53,
1958-59, 1959-60, 1973-74, 1984-85, 1990-91, 1991-92,
1992-93, 1993-94, 1997-98, 1998-99, 2004-05, 2005-06,
2008-09, 2009-10, 2010-11, 2012-13, 2014-15, 2015-16, 2017-18

COPA DEL REY
1909-10, 1911-12, 1912-13, 1919-20, 1921-22, 1924-25, 1925-26,
1927-28, 1941-42, 1950-51, 1951-52, 1952-53, 1956-57, 1958-59,
1962-63, 1967-68, 1970-71, 1977-78, 1980-81, 1982-83,
1987-88, 1989-90, 1996-97, 1997-98, 2008-09,
2011-12, 2014-15, 2015-16, 2016-17, 2017-18

SPANISH SUPER CUP
1983, 1991, 1992, 1994, 1996, 2005, 2006, 2009,
2010, 2011, 2013, 2016

SPANISH LEAGUE CUP
1982-83, 1985-86

SMALL WORLD CUP
1957

LATIN CUP
1949, 1952

PYRENEES CUP
1910, 1911, 1912, 1913

MEDITERRANEAN LEAGUE
1937

CATALAN LEAGUE
1937-38

CATALAN LEAGUE CHAMPIONSHIP
1901-02, 1902-03, 1904-05, 1908-09, 1909-10, 1910-11,
1912-13, 1915-16, 1918-19, 1919-20, 1920-21, 1921-22, 1923-24,
1924-25, 1925-26, 1926-27, 1927-28, 1929-30, 1930-31,
1931-32, 1934-35, 1935-36, 1937-38 (includes Copa
Macaya 1901-02 & Copa Barcelona 1902-03)

CATALAN SUPER CUP
2014-15

CATALAN CUP
1990-91, 1992-93, 1999-2000, 2003-04, 2004-05, 2006-07,
2012-13, 2013-14 (until 1993-94, Copa Generalitat)

EVA DUARTE CUP
1948-49, 1951-52, 1952-53